The Swear Word

Coloring Book

You Probably Need This One, Too

Tear-out pages, ready to frame!

Mommy Drinks

Because You Cry

A Sarcastic Coloring Book

The Swear Word

Coloring
Book

ST. MARTIN'S GRIFFIN
NEW YORK

ZENDOODLE COLORING PRESENTS THE SWEAR WORD COLORING BOOK.
Copyright © 2016 by St. Martin's Press. All rights reserved.
Printed in the United States of America. For information, address
St. Martin's Press, 175 Fifth Avenue, New York, N.Y. 10010.

THE SWEAR WORD COLORING BOOK is a compilation of materials published
in the volumes CHILL THE F*CK OUT and COLOR ME F*CKING CALM.

www.stmartins.com

ISBN 978-1-250-12064-9 (trade paperback)

Our books may be purchased in bulk for promotional, educational,
or business use. Please contact your local bookseller or the
Macmillan Corporate and Premium Sales Department at
1-800-221-7945, extension 5442, or by e-mail
at MacmillanSpecialMarkets@macmillan.com.

First Edition: May 2016

10 9 8 7 6 5 4 3 2 1

Simon says
go fuck yourself!

DON'T FUCK WITH ME

You say I'm a bitch

like it's a bad thing.

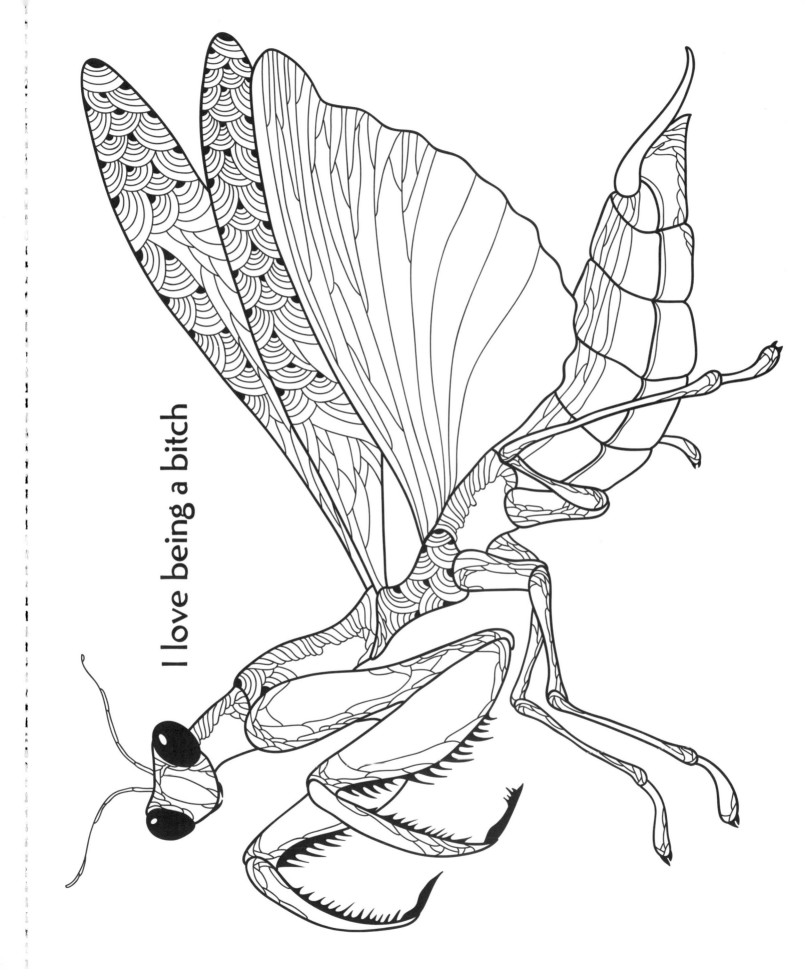

I love being a bitch

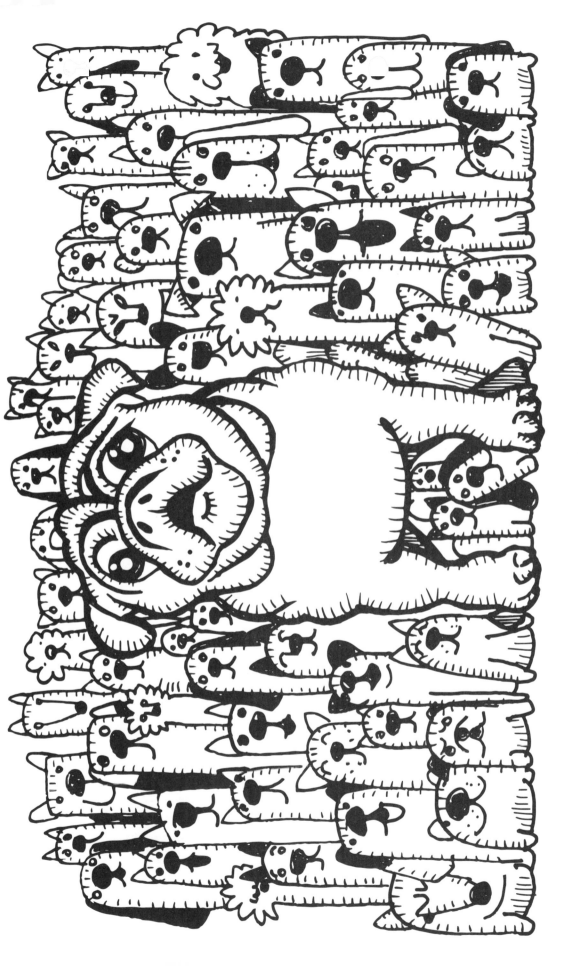

BAD BITCHES ONLY

Walk it off, pussy

Admitting you're an asshole is the first step

Have a nice day, asshole

LEAVE ME THE FUCK ALONE

CUT THE SHIT

FANCY AS FUCK

I fucking love you

Bullshit!

DO I LOOK LIKE SOMEONE WHO GIVES A SHIT?

DON'T LIKE
MY ATTITUDE?
★ CALL ★
1-800-FUCK-OFF

Total fucking
shitshow

Who gives a shit?

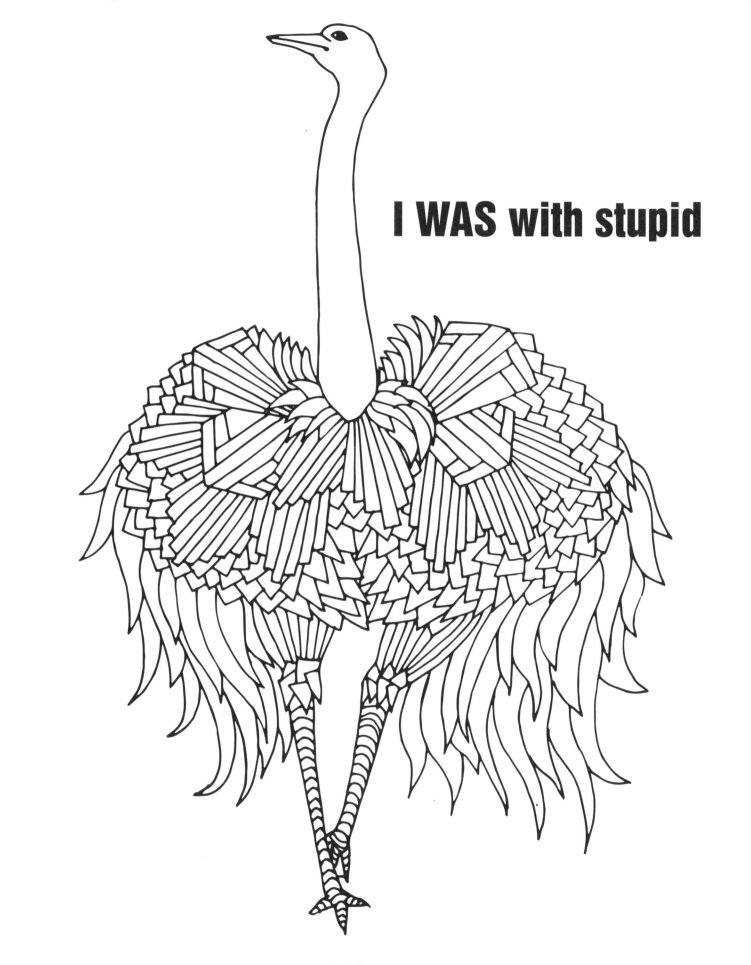

I WAS with stupid

NO SHIT,
Sherlock

Calm the fuck down

TRY NOT TO BE SUCH A DOUCHEBAG

I'm not always a bitch.
Just kidding—go fuck yourself.

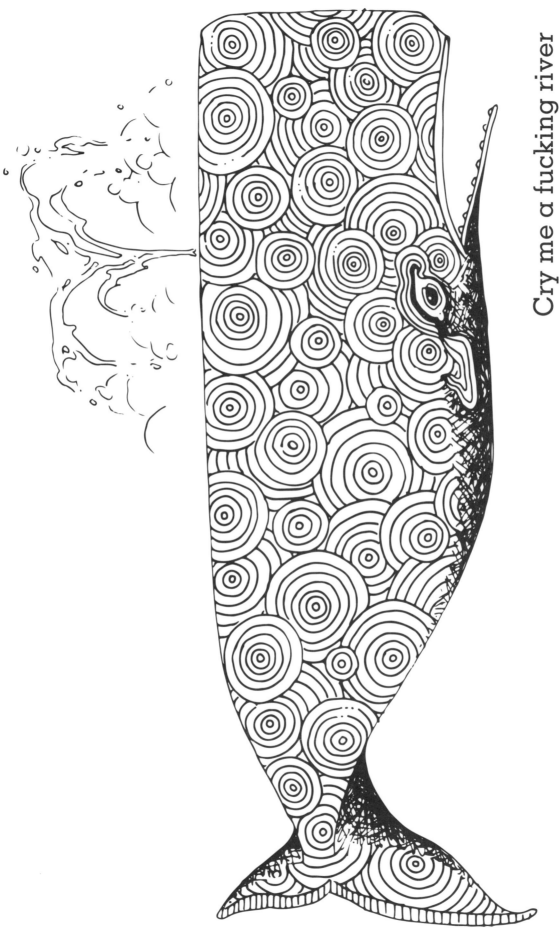

Cry me a fucking river

Queen of fucking

Everything

I hate
everyone
but you

Don't hate me because I'm fucking beautiful

BOSS BITCH

DOUCHE BAG

Just not yours.

Yes, I'm a bitch.

Fuck that shit

Ever think of that, fucker?

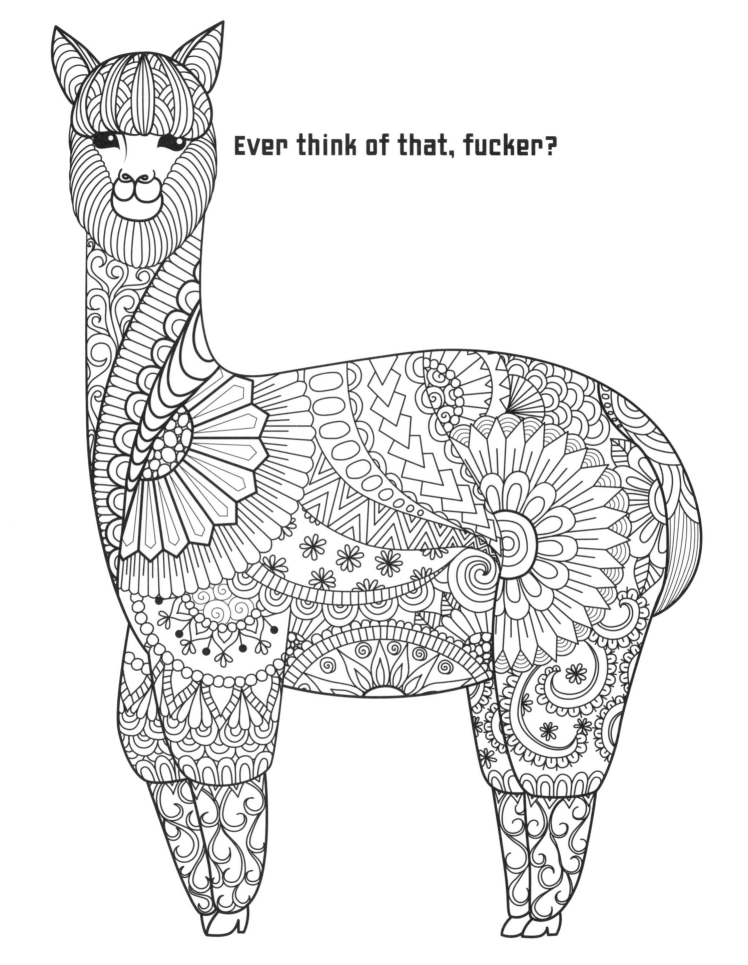

I'm the nicest asshole you'll ever meet

Let's play hide-and-go-fuck-yourself

I HAVE
NO FUCKS
TO GIVE.

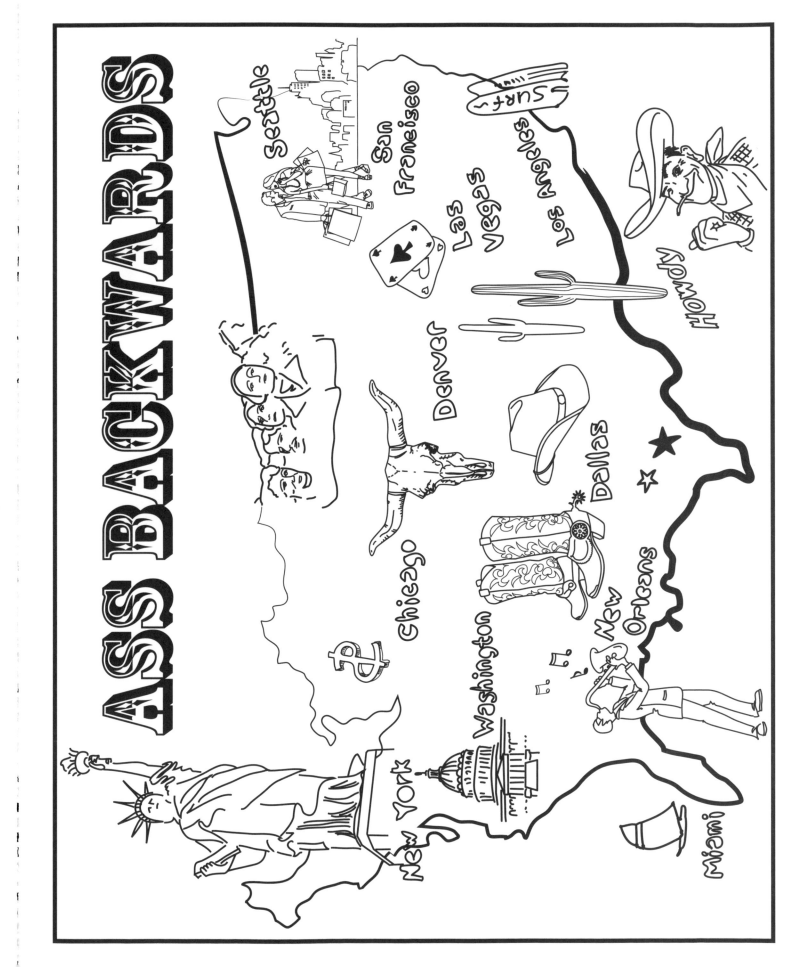

Smartass

Jackass

NAMASTE, BITCHES